P9-DDI-131

DISCARD

THE DRY DESERT

A Web of Life

Philip Johansson

Enslow Publishers, Inc.

40 Industrial Road   PO Box 38
Box 398
Berkeley Heights, NJ 07922   Hants GU12 6BP
USA   Aldershot

http://www.enslow.com

Library of Congress Cataloging-in-Publication Data

Johansson, Philip.
    The dry desert : a web of life / Philip Johansson.
       p. cm. — (A world of biomes)
    Includes index.
    Contents: Life in the slow lane — The desert biome — Desert communities —
    Desert plants — Desert animals.
    ISBN 0-7660-2200-5 (hardcover)
    1. Desert ecology-Juvenile literature. [1. Desert ecology. 2. Deserts. 3. Ecology.]
    I. Title II. Series: Johansson, Philip. World of biomes.
    QH541.5.D4J635 2004
    577.54-dc22

                           2003020443

Printed in the United States of America

10 9 8 7 6 5 4 3 2 1

To Our Readers: We have done our best to make sure all Internet Addresses in this book were active and appropriate when we went to press. However, the author and the publisher have no control over and assume no liability for the material available on those Internet sites or on other Web sites they may link to. Any comments or suggestions can be sent by e-mail to comments@enslow.com or to the address on the back cover.

Photo Credits: © 1999 Artville, LLC, pp. 10–11; © Cece Fabbro, pp. 7, 9; © Corel Corporation, pp. 17, 22, 37, 40; © D. Suzio/Photo Researchers, Inc., p. 4; © David Matherly/Visuals Unlimited, pp. 27, 34; © Gianni Tortoli/Photo Researchers, Inc., p. 19; © Gorge Ranalli/Photo Researchers, Inc., p. 15; © Jim Merli/Visuals Unlimited, p. 42; © Joe McDonald/Visuals Unlimited, p. 39; © John and Barbara Gerlach/Visuals Unlimited, p. 43; © John Cunningham/Visuals Unlimited, p. 32; Living Desert.org, pp. 29, 30, 31, 33; © Richard R. Hansen/Photo Researchers, Inc., p. 36; © Rick and Nora Bowers/Visuals Unlimited, pp. 38, 44; © Stephen Dalton/Photo Researchers, Inc., p. 41 (top); © Steve Maslowski/Visuals Unlimited, p. 41 (bottom); © Theo Allofs/Visuals Unlimited, pp. 13 (bottom), 20; © V. Engelbert/Photo Researchers, Inc., p. 13 (top).

Illustration Credits: *Heck's Pictorial Archive of Art and Architecture*, except for Dover Publications, Inc., pp. 5, 12, 21, 26, 35.

Cover Photos: © Corel Corporation (bottom right), © Jim Merli/Visuals Unlimited (bottom left), © Ken Lucas/Visuals Unlimited (top left), © Rick and Nora Bowers/Visuals Unlimited (top right).

Dr. Harold Avery is a conservation biologist from Drexel University, specializing in the biology of turtles and tortoises. He is studying desert tortoises in the Mojave Desert with his colleagues Dr. James Spotila (Drexel University) and Dr. Justin Congdon (Arizona State University). The volunteers depicted in Chapter 1 are from Earthwatch Institute, a nonprofit organization. Earthwatch supports field science and conservation through the participation of the public. See www.earthwatch.org for more information.

Table of
CONTENTS

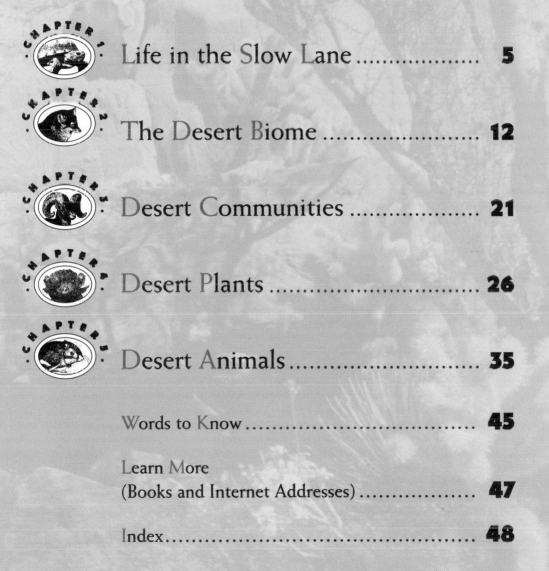

The desert tortoise lives in deserts of the southwestern United States.

LIFE *in the* SLOW LANE

Desert tortoises

can live for a year without food or water.
These slow-moving reptiles live in the
deserts of the southwestern United
States. They spend much of their time
in burrows, and creep across the dry land
in search of grasses and herbs to eat.
Dr. Harold Avery is trying to learn how
desert tortoises make the most of the
desert environment.

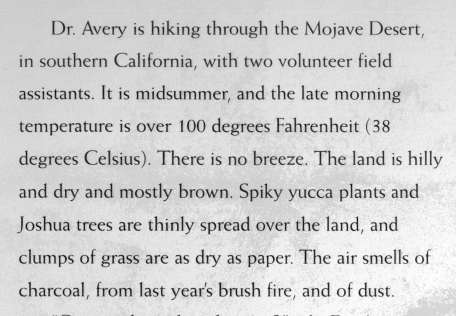

Dr. Avery is hiking through the Mojave Desert, in southern California, with two volunteer field assistants. It is midsummer, and the late morning temperature is over 100 degrees Fahrenheit (38 degrees Celsius). There is no breeze. The land is hilly and dry and mostly brown. Spiky yucca plants and Joshua trees are thinly spread over the land, and clumps of grass are as dry as paper. The air smells of charcoal, from last year's brush fire, and of dust.

"Can you hear that chirping?" asks Dr. Avery. He is holding an antenna in the air, connected to an electronic receiver hanging on his belt. The beeping of the receiver means that a tortoise is within range. The tortoise is wired with a transmitter that sends the chirping signal. Dr. Avery swings the antenna around in an arc to close in on the direction. "It's over that way."

The assistants search around the sparse, low plants until one of them finds the burrow. In the shade of the hole, a tortoise eyes them with concern.

Tortoises Inside and Out

After the tortoise is gently pulled out of her burrow, the assistants place her in the shade of a Joshua tree. They make sure that the transmitter glued to the tortoise's shell is still in good shape. One of them records the identity number painted on her shell and the location where they found her.

The other assistant measures the tortoise with a large device called a caliper. She looks closely for signs of disease, such as white lines on the animal's shell and runny eyes or nose.

"We caught this one last year," says Dr. Avery. "She's still in good health. Let's see if she's going to have young this year."

Dr. Avery starts a small generator with the yank of a chord. It is hooked to an X-ray camera.

Dr. Harold Avery and his assistants study the desert tortoise.

The tortoise is placed under the camera, and everyone stands back while the camera is triggered. Later, the X-ray shows that this tortoise has four eggs inside her, soon to be laid. She is not only surviving in this barren-looking stretch of land, she is making more tortoises.

Learning From Tortoises

Dr. Avery has been studying desert tortoises in the Mojave Desert for twelve years. He wants to learn how tortoises respond to changes in the desert environment. For example, how will a change in rain patterns affect their survival? Knowing this will help land managers protect desert tortoises and other sensitive animals and plants that live in the desert.

Deserts are unique environments. Although they may look empty and bare, they are full of many interesting plants and animals. Scientists like Dr. Avery study how desert plants and animals live together.

Dr. Avery's
assistant lets
the tortoise go.

What Is a Biome?

The desert is one kind of biome. A biome is a large region of the earth where certain forms of plants and animals live. They survive there because they are well suited to the climate found in that area. Climate is the temperatures and amounts of rainfall that usually occur during a year.

Each biome supports plants that may not be found in other biomes. Large trees grow in forests, but not in deserts. Cacti grow in deserts, but not in the tundra. The different animals that eat these different plants help form the living communities of a biome. Exploring biomes is a good way to understand

LEGEND

- Tundra
- Taiga
- Temperate forest
- Grassland
- Desert
- Rain forest
- Chaparral
- Mountain zone
- Polar ice

Biomes

how these communities work. In this book you will learn about the things that make the desert special, and about the plants and animals that live in this biome.

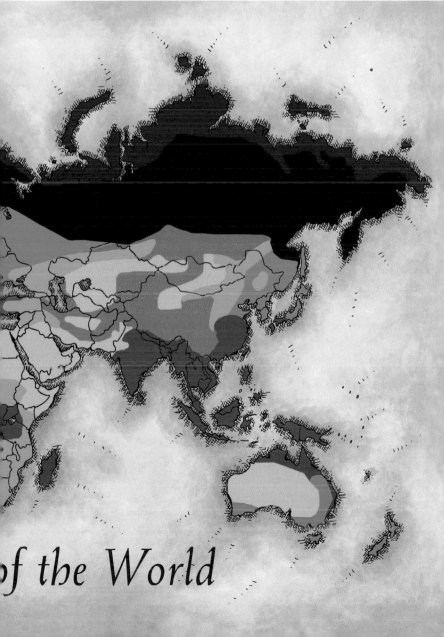

of the World

The DESERT BIOME

Deserts cover one fifth of the world's land surface. They can be found on every continent except Europe. The largest desert is the Sahara Desert in Africa. It covers 3.5 million square miles (9.1 million square kilometers). This desert covers nearly one third the area of Africa.

Deserts arc the driest places on Earth. Walking through one, you feel the full heat of the sun because there are no clouds and no tall trees for shade. The air is usually dry and dusty. Tough, spiny plants growing low to the ground can scratch your leg. You may see some unusual animals, although most of them are active in the cooler hours of the evening.

Many people picture deserts as miles and miles of drifting sand dunes, with little life. There are some deserts like that, but most of them are full of interesting plants and animals. Every desert is

Although many people think of deserts as stretches of dunes, most deserts are filled with plant and animal life.

different. Some, such as the Sonoran Desert of the southwestern United States, even have as many different plants and animals as found in forests.

Desert Weather

Most deserts get less than ten inches (twenty-five centimeters) of rain per year. That is a third of the precipitation that forests need to grow. The driest deserts, the Atacama Desert of Chile and the central Sahara, get only about half an inch (one and a half centimeters) of rain each year. They may even go a year or two without any rain.

Desert rainfall usually comes in short downpours. These can be at any time, but in some deserts the rain comes seasonally. All desert plants and animals live for the coming of the rain. Most of them wait to flower or mate until after the seasonal rain, when water is not as scarce.

Evaporation makes deserts even drier. During evaporation, water changes from liquid into water vapor. Moisture leaves the land under the desert sun and goes into the dry desert air. More moisture could evaporate from a desert than could fall as rain or snow. In some deserts, rain can evaporate before it even hits the ground.

Deserts can be amazingly hot during the day. In many other biomes, such as forests, air filled with

A desert rain does not come often. After the rain, many plants will flower.

A desert night can be much cooler than the day. Temperatures are sometimes as low as 20 degrees Fahrenheit (−7 degrees Celsius).

moisture covers the land like a blanket. But in most deserts, with very little moist air and no tall trees, the surface gets twice as much of the sun's heat. Temperatures above 100 degrees Fahrenheit (38 degrees Celsius) are not uncommon, and extremes of 120 degrees Fahrenheit (50 degrees Celsius) are possible.

At night, the missing blanket of moist air allows the heat to leave the desert twice as quickly. Temperatures can drop down to 20 degrees Fahrenheit (−7 degrees Celsius) in the winter, and may even reach as low as 0 degrees Fahrenheit (−18 degrees Celsius) in some deserts.

Deserts are generally warm or hot, with an average temperature in the 70s Fahrenheit (20s Celsius). Many deserts rarely experience a frost. But several deserts may have extended periods of below-freezing temperatures. It might even snow during the winter. Examples of these "cold deserts" are the Great Basin Desert of the western United States, the Taklimakan of western China, and the Iranian Desert.

A Parched Land

Since there is not much moisture in the desert, the soil there is different from the soil of other biomes. Most desert soils are made of sand, gravel, and rocks. These coarse desert soils allow good drainage. Most of the rain that hits the ground sinks beneath it quickly. Seasonal ponds, puddles, and streams may appear after a rain, but permanent bodies of surface water, such as lakes, are not common.

Some deserts have rivers running through them. The Sahara has the Nile River, and the American Southwest has the Rio Grande. Other desert water is stored deep below the soil. This underground water may spring to the surface, such as in the oases of the Sahara.

The extremely dry climate of deserts poses a challenge for the plants and animals that live in them. The abundance of energy from the sun in the desert

In some deserts, water is stored beneath the ground. When the water comes up to the surface, a desert oasis forms.

provides for many forms of life. But these life-forms must be able to survive the lack of water.

✓ **Hot and cold:**
Temperatures are
generally warm,
averaging in the
70s Fahrenheit
(20s Celsius).
Temperatures
commonly reach over
100 degrees Fahrenheit
(38 degrees Celsius).
But some deserts are
"cold," experiencing
extended periods below
freezing during the winter.

DESERT FACTS

✓ **No blanket:**
The lack of humidity
in the desert air
results in more of
the sun's energy
reaching the ground
during the day.
Likewise, the lack
of insulation allows
more heat to
leave the ground
during the night.

✓ **Low precipitation:** Usually
less than ten inches (twenty-five
centimeters) of precipitation fall each
year.

✓ **High evaporation:**
Potential evaporation—the turning
from liquid water into water vapor—
exceeds precipitation. Some rainfall
evaporates before it hits the ground.

✓ **Dry soil:** Desert soils are
coarse—mostly sand, gravel, and
rocks—and dry.

✓ **Where's the water?** Surface
water does not last long in the desert.
Deserts may have seasonal streams or
ponds, and some have rivers running
through them, but most desert land is
dry most of the year.

DESERT COMMUNITIES

Like every other biome, the desert is made up of living communities of plants and animals. Communities are the groups of living things found together in a place. Within a community, some plants and animals depend on others. Each living thing has a role in the community.

A cactus gathers energy from the sun through its green stems.

Energy Flow in the Desert

Plants, such as cacti and sagebrush, trap energy from sunlight for their food. Since they have no leaves, cacti soak in the sun's energy through the surface of their green stems. They use the energy to make sugar from carbon dioxide (a gas in the air) and the water from the soil. They later use the energy in the sugars to build new leaves, stems, roots, and flowers.

Some animals, such as desert bighorn sheep and grasshoppers, eat these plants. Animals that eat only plants are called herbivores. Herbivores get their energy from plants. Other animals, called carnivores, eat herbivores. Coyotes, vultures, and zebra-tailed lizards are carnivores.

SUNLIGHT

↓ USED BY

PLANTS 〰〰 HEAT LOSS

↓ EATEN BY

HERBIVORES 〰〰 HEAT LOSS

↓ EATEN BY

CARNIVORES 〰〰 HEAT LOSS

SOIL LIFE
(decomposers)

At each stage in the flow of energy through the desert community, some energy is lost as heat.

Carnivores get their energy from eating the meat of other animals. Some animals, such as roadrunners, eat both plants and animals. They are called omnivores.

When plants and animals die, soil animals and fungi help break them down. These animals are called decomposers. This releases nutrients back into the soil.

The Food Web

Energy flows through the desert from the sun to plants to herbivores to carnivores to decomposers. The energy flow follows a pattern called a food web. The food web connects the plants and animals of a biome. It shows who eats whom. For instance, lizards eat insects. Roadrunners eat lizards. Coyotes eat roadrunners.

Together, plants and animals pass energy through the biome community. They also use some of the energy to live. At each stage of the food web, some energy is lost as the animals use it. It is lost in the form of heat. More energy from the sun has to be trapped by plants to keep the community alive.

Learning from Biomes

Exploring biomes such as the desert is a good way to learn how living communities work. By looking at the plants and animals in any biome, you will see how they all need each other. If you take any plant or animal away, it could change how the community works.

SOME PLANTS AND ANIMALS IN THE
DESERT FOOD WEB

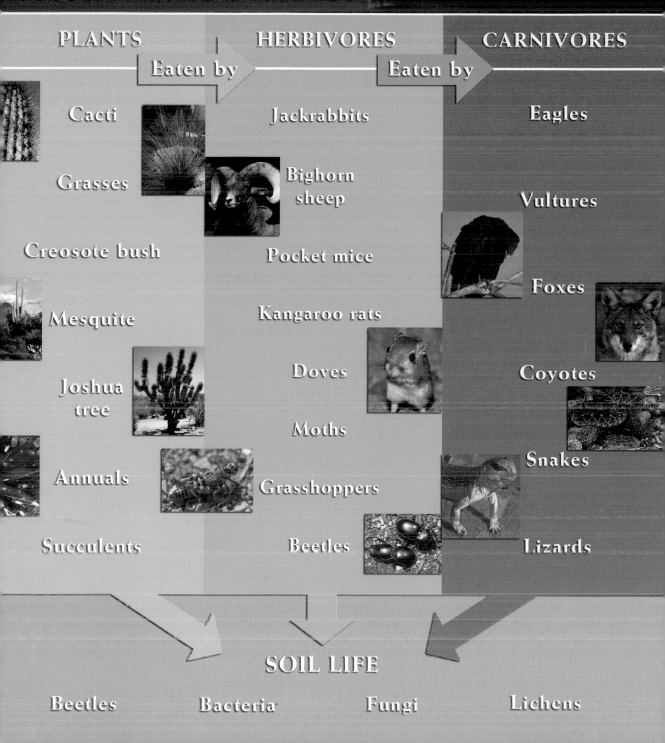

PLANTS	HERBIVORES	CARNIVORES
Eaten by →	*Eaten by* →	
Cacti	Jackrabbits	Eagles
Grasses	Bighorn sheep	Vultures
Creosote bush	Pocket mice	Foxes
Mesquite	Kangaroo rats	Coyotes
Joshua tree	Doves	
Annuals	Moths	Snakes
Succulents	Grasshoppers	Lizards
	Beetles	

SOIL LIFE

Beetles   Bacteria   Fungi   Lichens

·DESERT PLANTS·

Chapter 4

DESERT PLANTS

Some deserts,

like the central Sahara, are so hot and dry that nothing can grow there. But most deserts have many kinds of plants. These may include cacti, shrubs, grasses, and short trees. If you were to walk through the desert, you would notice that most desert plants look tough and spiny and scratchy.

◈ **26** ◈

The Sonoran Desert in Arizona is filled with many different kinds of plants.

A Joshua tree can grow as tall as 30 feet (10 meters).

Desert plants usually do not grow very tall, because of the lack of water. Most are no taller than a person. They do not form a canopy overhead, as do trees in moist forests. The Joshua tree of the Mojave Desert, where desert tortoises live, may grow as tall as 30 feet (10 meters). But they grow far apart from each other. Saguaros, the giant cacti of the Sonoran Desert, cast very little shadow with their fleshy stems. The only shade in the Sonoran is from low paloverde and ironwood trees. Again, these grow far apart from each other.

There is lots of room between desert plants. The bare ground around them is home to nearly invisible fungi and lichens. Lichens are part fungi and part algae. It is also home to wildflowers and grasses, which may cover the desert floor after a seasonal rain.

Saving Water

Desert plants have unusual shapes to deal with the lack of water. They have unique ways to

collect water. Many desert plants, such as cacti, have a large net of roots that spreads over the ground. These roots collect as much water as possible after the rare rain.

Other plants, like a low-growing tree called mesquite, have deep taproots that reach 20 to 30 feet (6 to 9 meters) down. They can reach water stored deep beneath the ground.

Many desert plants also store water in unusual ways. Cacti store water in the

◇ **29** ◇

The agave plant holds water in its fleshy leaves.

The spines of ➤ a cactus protect the plant from many animals that might want to eat it.

spongy tissue of their stems, so they can survive most of the year without rain. Their stems swell when they are full of water after a rain. Many other desert plants, such as agaves and aloes, have fleshy leaves that store water. Others store water in their roots.

Desert plants need to be able to hold on to their stored water. Otherwise the severe heat and drying wind of the desert can dry out the plants. Plants often have small, thick leaves, with less surface area from which to lose water. Leaves have a waxy coating to keep them from drying out. Some plants even lose their leaves for the driest part of the year, so they do not lose water from the leaves' surface.

Cacti do not have any leaves—they have spines instead. Cacti soak in the sun's energy through the surface of their green stem. The spines protect them from many animals that may want to eat their watery flesh. Plants called euphorbias, which grow in deserts of Africa and Asia, look very similar to cacti. They also have spines to protect their water-storing flesh.

After the Rain

For most of the year, the desert changes little. Desert plants live off stored water and wait for the next rain. Many deserts have a short season of rains, which brings a new burst of life to desert plants. Shrubs that lost their leaves grow them again, desert grasses have new green growth, and annual plants cover the desert floor.

Annual plants, like desert sand verbena, spend most of the year in the form of seeds with a hard coating. When the rains come, they quickly emerge from their seeds, reach out of the ground, and flower. They finish their life cycle, making next year's seeds, all in about three weeks.

Perennial plants survive underground

After a rain, the desert sand verbena will grow and flower in three short weeks.

in the form of bulbs or roots most of the year. These plants, such as the pink-flowered bitterroot of North American sagebrush deserts, also come to life after the rain. Most other desert plants, from cacti to creosote bushes, flower after the rain. They fill the desert with their scents and colors for a short period.

A cactus flowers after the rain.

The desert is a challenging place for plants to grow. The variety of desert plants forms a special environment for animals of the desert. Despite their tough, spiny nature, desert plants collect enough energy to support the many animals of the desert food web.

No canopy:

Because the lack of water cannot support large, leafy trees, desert plants are low growing and do not form a canopy overhead.

Ready roots:

Desert plants have roots designed to collect water from infrequent rains. The roots are either large nets on the desert floor or deep taproots that reach deep into the ground.

Flower season:

Most desert plants flower just after the seasonal rains, giving the desert a short-lived burst of color.

PLANTS FACTS

Sealed in:

Plants in the desert limit their water loss by having small, thick leaves with a waxy coating. Some shrubs lose their leaves in the driest part of the year, and cacti have no leaves at all.

Short life:

Annual plants remain as seeds for most of the year, only springing up after a seasonal rain. They live the rest of their life cycle, growing and flowering, in a matter of three weeks.

Water storage:

Desert plants store rainwater in their stems, fleshy leaves, or roots.

DESERT ANIMALS

Animals in the desert face many of the same challenges as desert plants. It can be very hot in the desert, and water is extremely scarce. These hardships limit the activities of some animals. They have also led to unusual ways to store water. A variety of fascinating animals have developed adaptations to help them live in the desert.

A kangaroo rat is one of the nocturnal rodents of the desert biome.

Escaping the Heat

One of the most common adaptations of desert animals is being nocturnal. This means they are active during the night, rather than in the heat of day. Nocturnal animals avoid the strong sun and dry air during the day to keep from drying out.

During the day the desert is quiet, with only a few insects, reptiles, and birds active. But at night the desert is lively. All kinds of small mammals come out in search of seeds and plants to eat. Kangaroo rats, pack rats, pocket mice, and jackrabbits scamper over well-used trails in deserts of the southwestern United States. Predators, such as foxes, coyotes, and sidewinder snakes,

also emerge at night to hunt the small mammals. Bats come out to hunt flying insects. These carnivores continue the desert food web.

Many small mammals live in burrows or dens. Tunnels under the ground give them a cool place to sleep through the heat of the day. Reptiles and amphibians such as desert tortoises, rattlesnakes, and coral snakes also live in burrows. They may come out to bask in the sun during the day, to warm their blood. But they will also go back to their burrows if it is too hot or for protection from daytime predators like Swainson's hawks. There are so many burrowing animals in the desert that they often share burrows or reuse those that were abandoned by other animals.

The sidewinder snake hunts for its food in the desert.

An elf owl lives inside a cactus. It comes out at night.

Some desert birds are nocturnal. Elf owls emerge from their roosts within saguaro cacti at night. The common nighthawk hunts for flying insects in the dark. But most birds are active in the day, especially early morning or early evening. White-winged doves feed on seeds, and cactus wrens search for insects. Their naturally high body temperatures and insulating coat of feathers help them stand the daytime heat.

Saving Water

Some desert animals never drink water. The kangaroo rat of the Sonoran Desert gets all the water it needs from the seeds it eats. The addax, an antelope of the

Sahara Desert, follows the occasional rains in search of fresh grasses for their moisture. All desert animals need to conserve water, to keep from losing the water in their bodies. For instance, desert animals have more concentrated urine, so they do not lose so much water when they excrete waste.

Most desert animals are small. There are not as many large mammals in the desert as there are in other habitats. It is easier to conserve enough water to keep a small body alive than a large one. It is also easier for smaller animals to find shelter from the desert sun, in burrows or in the shade of desert shrubs. There are some exceptions, such as the Sahara's addax and the Mojave's coyote and bighorn sheep. These animals are able to survive on the scarce food and water found in the desert.

Some larger mammals, such as the bighorn sheep, can survive the harsh conditions of the desert.

The desert iguana's watertight skin does not allow water to be lost from its body.

Insects, such ▶ as the desert locust, can eat the new plants that grow after the rain falls.

Roadrunners ▶ eat small desert animals.

Insects and reptiles are especially well suited for living in the desert. Insects, such as grasshoppers, and reptiles, such as desert iguanas, have watertight skins. Unlike mammals, they do not lose water from their body surface. They secrete even more concentrated urine than other desert animals, in the form of uric acid. This saves water. These special features are why there are many kinds of insects and reptiles in the desert. It is also why they can be active through the heat of the day.

The Desert Year

Like desert plants, many desert animals spend their lives waiting for the next rain. In some deserts the rain comes seasonally, but in others it comes at any time, if at all. The rain is followed

by fresh growth of annuals and other plants. Abundant insects, such as grasshoppers, moths, and ants, feed on the new growth and flower nectar. Reptiles, such as zebra-tailed lizards, chuckwallas, and other lizards, feed on the many insects. So do desert birds, like cactus wrens and curve-billed thrashers of the Sonoran Desert. Some birds, like the roadrunner, eat small reptiles.

The burst of plant growth is also a bonus for burrowing rodents These mammals stock up on extra seeds and fatten up during this time. They also have babies and feed them the new food. Foxes, coyotes, snakes, golden eagles, and other predators in turn enjoy the growing numbers of small mammals to eat.

In the time after the rains, all desert animals

store extra fat. This excess helps them get through the lean months ahead. Some animals have adaptations for

The venomous Gila monster stores fat in its tail. It can use the fat during times when food is not available.

storing fat. Gila monsters—brightly patterned, venomous lizards of the Sonoran Desert—store loads of fat in their plump tail to help them survive long periods without food. The fat sand rat of the Arabian Desert is similar to a gerbil, but it has a thick layer of fat to overcome the long droughts and lack of food.

Some desert animals are active only after the rains. Many insects lay eggs that hatch only after a rain. Amphibians, which must develop in water, lay eggs and develop into adults very quickly. This speedy growth takes advantage of short-lived puddles or trickles of streams. Some amphibians, like the spadefoot toad,

spend as much as nine months underground, only coming out after the rains.

The desert tortoises that Dr. Harold Avery studies are active throughout the year. But like other desert creatures, they rely on the rare rainfall that keeps the herbs and grasses they eat alive. Dr. Avery's work will help biologists understand how the Mojave Desert animals, including desert tortoises, survive in such a dry climate.

The desert biome is surprisingly full of life, especially after rain. The living community found in the desert survives despite extreme temperatures and very dry conditions. These plants and animals make up the food web that brings the desert to life.

The spadefoot toad emerges from the desert ground after a rain.

ANIMAL FACTS

✓ **Nocturnal habits:** Many desert animals are active at night to avoid the heat and dry air of the daytime. Even animals that are active in the day take a rest at midday.

✓ **Living underground:** Reptiles, amphibians, mammals, and insects burrow underground to escape the heat of the day.

✓ **Small is helpful:** Desert animals tend to be small because they need less water. Large mammals are less common in the desert than in other habitats.

✓ **Waterproof skin:** Insects and reptiles have watertight outer layers. They also have other adaptations for conserving water, such as concentrated urine.

✓ **Living for rain:** Many animals have life cycles tied to the uncommon rains. Most reproduce after the rain.

✓ **Surviving the famine:** Desert animals fatten up during times of plenty to survive the long periods of little food.

WORDS TO KNOW

adaptation—A trait of a plant or animal that helps it to live under certain conditions.

annual—A plant that goes through an entire life cycle in one year, growing from a seed, flowering, making its own seeds, and dying.

biome—An area of the earth defined by the kinds of plants that live there.

caliper—A measuring device with two arms and a ruler, used to measure thickness or diameter.

canopy—The area where the tops of the trees come together and block the sunlight.

carnivore—An animal that eats other animals.

climate—The average weather conditions in an area, usually measured over years. It includes temperature, precipitation, and wind speeds.

community—All the plants and animals living and interacting in any area.

decomposers—Soil animals and fungi that help break down dead plants and animals, releasing nutrients back into the soil.

evaporation—The conversion of liquid water to water vapor.

food web—The connections that show the transfer of energy from the sun to plants to herbivores, carnivores, and decomposers.

herbivore—An animal that eats plants.

insulation—A substance that can trap heat, such as humid air that traps heat from the sun, acting like a blanket to keep Earth warm.

nocturnal—Active at night rather than during the day.

nutrients—Chemicals necessary for plants and animals to live and grow.

perennial—A plant that survives year after year, but may survive the winter or dry season in the form of bulbs or roots under the ground.

precipitation—Water falling in a given area in the form of rain, snow, or fog.

predator—An animal that hunts other animals for food.

succulent—A plant with thick, fleshy leaves or stems that store water from the infrequent rains.

taproot—A root that grows deep into the soil to reach water far below.

transmitter—A small electronic device that gives off a radio signal, used for tracking animals.

BOOKS

Arnosky, Jim. *Watching Desert Wildlife*. Washington, D.C.: National Geographic Society, 2002.

Brown, John. *Journey into the Desert*. New York: Oxford University Press, 2003.

Pfeffer, Wendy. *Hot Deserts*. New York: Benchmark Books, 2002.

Morris, Neil. *The Wonders of our World: Deserts*. New York: Crabtree Publishing Co., 1996.

Wright-Frierson, Virginia. *A Desert Scrapbook: Dawn to Dusk in the Sonoran Desert*. New York: Simon & Schuster, 2002.

INTERNET ADDRESSES

Missouri Botanical Garden. *Biomes of the World*. "Desert." http://mbgnet.mobot.org/sets/desert/

Woodward, Susan L. *Major Biomes of the World*. "Desertscrub." http://www.runet.edu/~swoodwar/CLASSES/GEOG235/biomes/desert/desert.html

INDEX